Second Edition

Learning World **1**
WORKBOOK

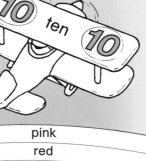

JN122213

pink
red
orange
yellow
green
blue
purple
brown
black
gray
white

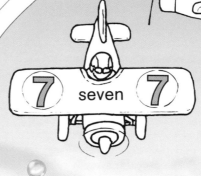

upper case

lower case

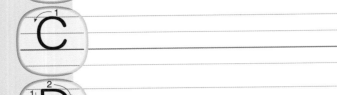

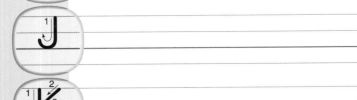

upper case

lower case

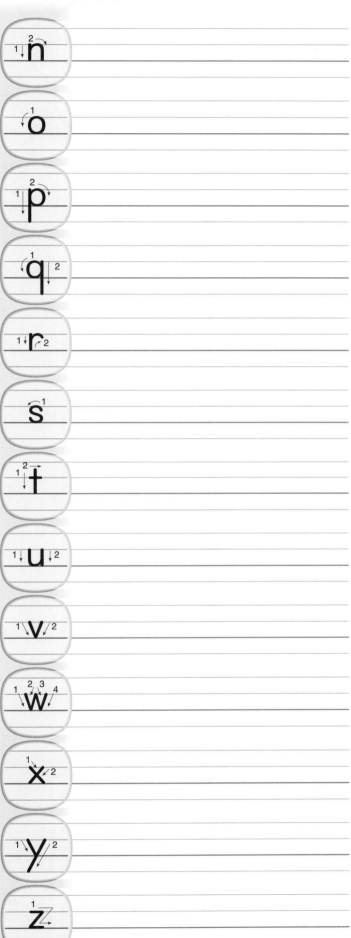

かきじゅんにきまりはありません。
このかきじゅんは１つのれいです。

1 Color and read.

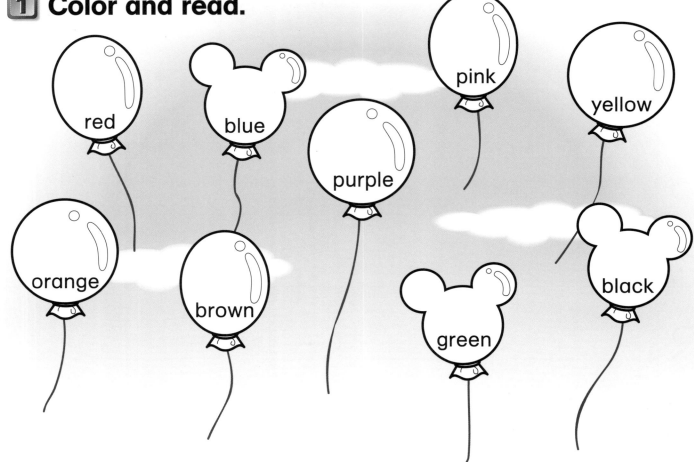

red
blue
purple
pink
yellow
orange
brown
green
black

2 How old are you?

I am eight years old.

I am six years old.

I am five years old.

1 one	2 two	3 three	4 four	5 five	6 six	7 seven	8 eight	9 nine	10 ten

1 Find their names.

Sara

Paul

Jamie

Nancy

2 What is your name?

My name is

My Family

Students draw the members of their family.
Ask each student while they are drawing: "Who's he (she)?" "What's his (her) name?"

1 Connect the stars and numbers.

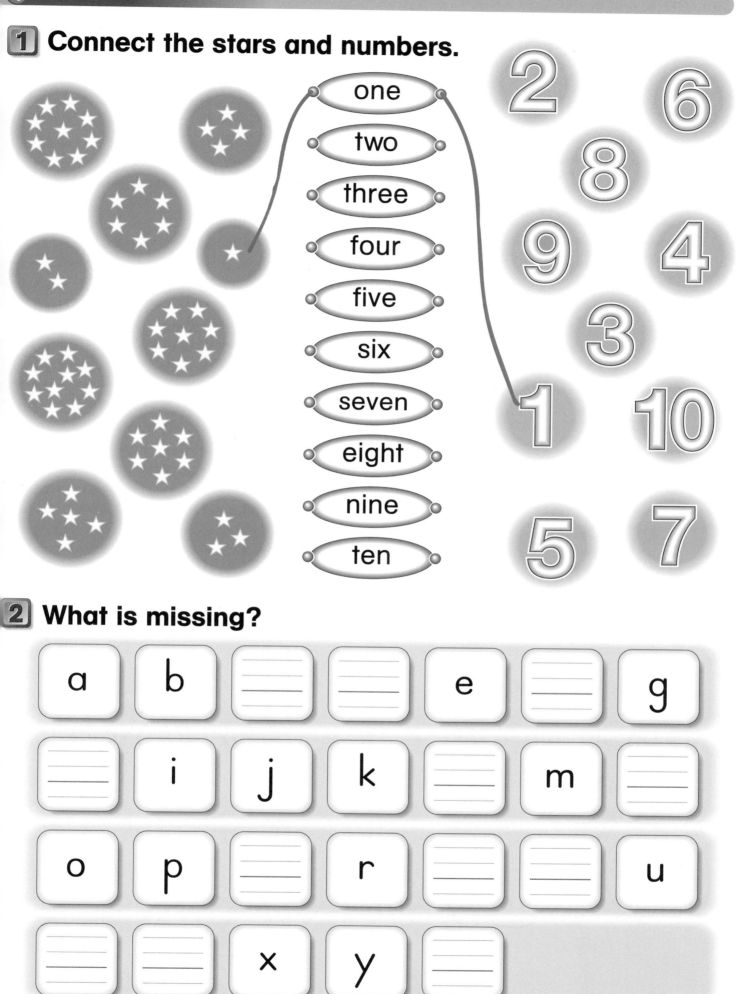

one
two
three
four
five
six
seven
eight
nine
ten

2 6
8
9 4
3
1 10
5 7

2 What is missing?

| a | b | ___ | ___ | e | ___ | g |

| ___ | i | j | k | ___ | m | ___ |

| o | p | ___ | r | ___ | ___ | u |

| ___ | ___ | x | y | ___ |

1 Let's color.

1 a big yellow car

2 a small blue car

3 a new red car

4 an old green car

big

old

small

new

2 Let's color.

1 a big black bike

2 a small pink bike

3 a new orange bike

4 an old purple bike

small

new

old

big

8

2

Let's color.

1 China
yellow ... red

2 U.S.A.
white ... red
blue ... white

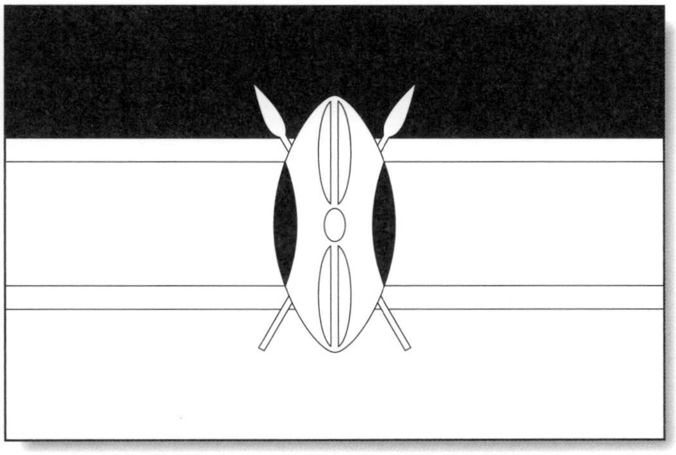

3 Kenya
black
white ... red
green ... white

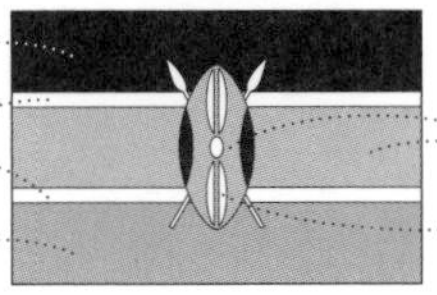

4 Germany
black
yellow ... red

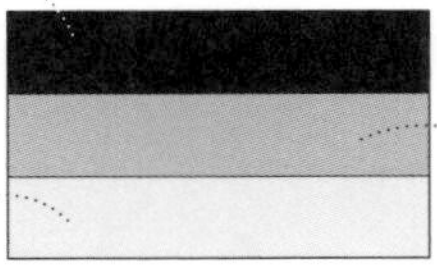

5 Thailand
... blue
red ... white

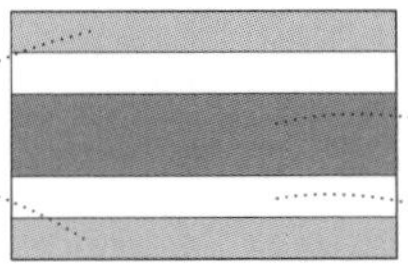

6 Japan
... red
white

9

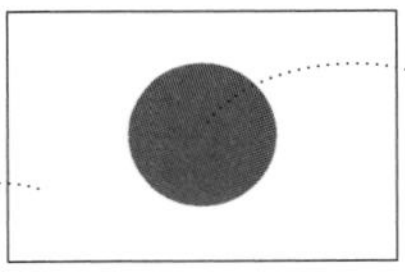

1 Draw.

① happy

② sad

③ angry

④ funny

2 Yes / No

①
Are you happy?

Yes   No

②
Are you angry?

Yes   No

③
Are you angry?

Yes   No

Connect the dots from a to z.

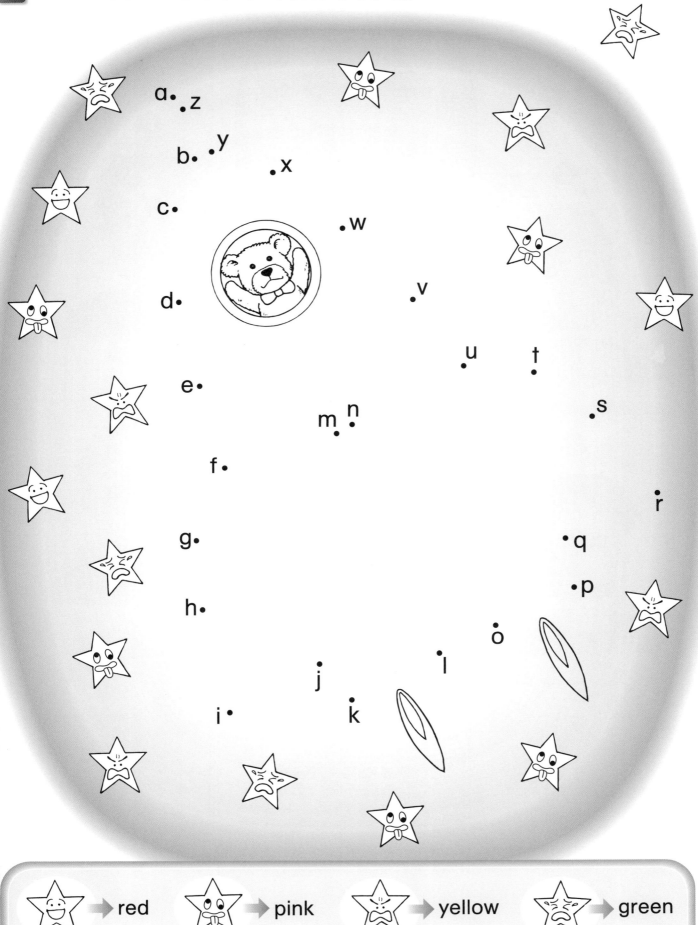

a. .z

b. .y

.x

c.

.w

d.

.v

.u   t

e.

s.

m. n

f.

.r

g.   .q

.p

h.   .o

.l

j

i.   k

red   pink   yellow   green

◯ What is missing?

eye(s) nose mouth ear(s) hair

1 How is the weather?

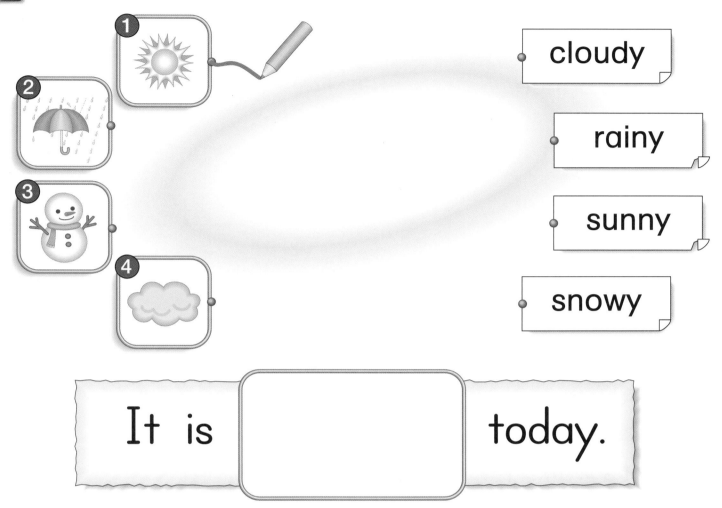

cloudy

rainy

sunny

snowy

It is _____ today.

2 Let's play with blocks. How many blocks?

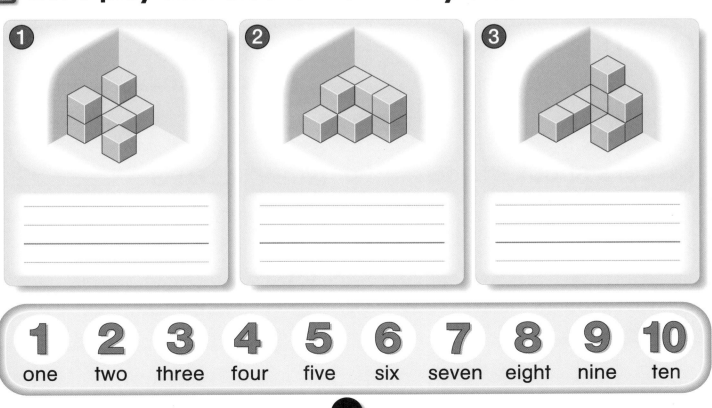

1	2	3	4	5	6	7	8	9	10
one	two	three	four	five	six	seven	eight	nine	ten

Connect the dots and write the words.

1 Let's dance.

Let's _____

2 Let's run.

Let's _____

3 Let's go.

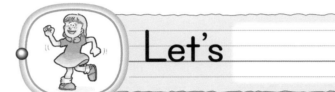
Let's _____

4 Let's walk.

Let's _____

5 Let's stop.

Let's _____

6 Let's shout.

Let's _____

7 Let's sing.

Let's _____

Word Search

1 blue   2 red   3 pink   4 purple

5 green   6 black   7 orange   8 brown

a	p	u	r	p	l	e
m	b	o	p	q	r	e
b	l	u	e	i	g	s
r	a	w	u	n	n	t
o	c	z	a	x	y	k
w	k	r	v	r	e	d
n	o	g	r	e	e	n

Look at the words in the box.
Find them in the puzzle and circle them with the correct colors.

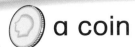 a coin  coins

1 Circle.

 ①   a coin   or   coins

 ②   a coin   or   coins

 ③   an umbrella   or   umbrellas

 ④   an umbrella   or   umbrellas

2 How many…?

① How many coins? 	
② How many desks? 	
③ How many umbrellas? 	

 **1** one   **2** two   **3** three   **4** four   **5** five   **6** six

1 Draw pictures.

1 a big yellow pumpkin

2 a small purple apple

3 a big blue apple

4 a small green pumpkin

5 a big pink eggplant

6 a small orange eggplant

pumpkin

apple

eggplant

2 Circle.

1 Do you have an apple?

Yes, I do.

No, I don't.

2 Do you have an eggplant?

Yes, I do.

No, I don't.

What time is it?

1 It's _____ o'clock.

5 It's _____ o'clock.

2 It's _____ o'clock.

6 It's _____ o'clock.

3 It's _____ o'clock.

7 It's _____ o'clock.

4 It's _____ o'clock.

8 It's _____ o'clock.

1	2	3	4	5	6	7	8	9	10	11	12
one	two	three	four	five	six	seven	eight	nine	ten	eleven	twelve

Connect the matching letters.

A   b

B   d

C   c

D   a

Write the letters.

A   a

B   b

C   c

D   d

Say the words, color and write.

Aa → blue   Bb → yellow   Cc → green   Dd → orange

 A a

 B b

 C c

 D d

1 <u>like</u> / <u>don't like</u>

① <u>I</u> _____ dogs

② <u>I</u> _____ snakes

③ <u>I</u> _____ cats

④ <u>I</u> _____ spiders

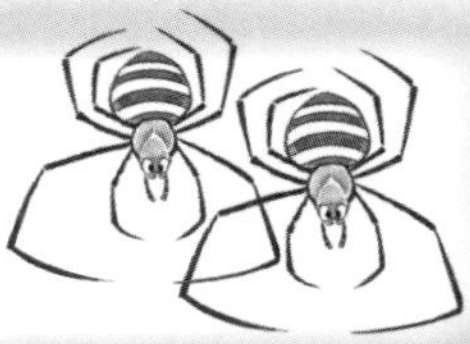

2 <u>Yes</u> / <u>No</u>

❶ Do you like snakes? _____

❷ Do you like dogs? _____

❸ Do you like spiders? _____

❹ Do you like cats? _____

1 Color the animals.

1 a yellow rabbit

2 a green hippo

3 an orange giraffe

4 a blue fox

5 a brown lion

6 a black bear

rabbit

lion

bear

hippo

giraffe

fox

2 Answer the questions.

1 What color is the hippo? _____

2 What color is the giraffe? _____

3 What color is the bear? _____

4 What color is the lion? _____

5 What color is the rabbit? _____

6 What color is the fox? _____

1 Color the ghosts.

❶ A yellow ghost is jumping.

❷ A green ghost is running.

❸ A brown ghost is walking.

❹ A blue ghost is sitting.

❺ A red ghost is flying.

❻ A black ghost is swimming.

❼ An orange ghost is sleeping.

2 Find the correct ghosts.

❶ A green ghost is _____

❷ A yellow ghost is _____

❸ A black ghost is _____

sleeping   swimming   flying   running   walking   sitting   jumping

Connect the matching letters.

E   h

F   g

G   f

H   e

Write the letters.

E   e

F   f

G   g

H   h

Say the words, color and write.

Ee → red   Ff → blue   Gg → yellow   Hh → green

 E e

 F f

 G g

 H h

1 Say the words and color.

1. spaghetti
2. salad
3. pancakes
4. pizza
5. cake
6. cheese
7. ice cream
8. apple pie

2 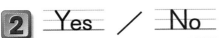 Yes / No

1	Do you want cake?	
2	Do you want pizza?	
3	Do you want ice cream?	
4	Do you want spaghetti?	
5	Do you want salad?	

1 Say the words and color.

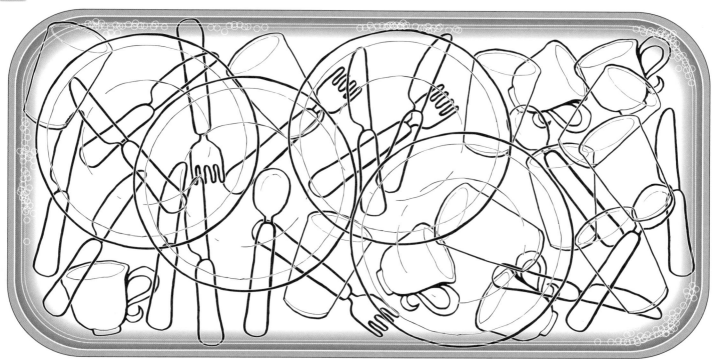

2 Answer the questions.

1 How many forks can you see? _____

2 How many plates can you see? _____

3 How many knives can you see? _____

4 How many spoons can you see? _____

5 How many glasses can you see? _____

6 How many cups can you see? _____

 plates cups  knives  spoons forks glasses

1 Color the pictures.

1 Color the **little apple red.**

2 Color the **big apple green.**

3 Color the **big bag yellow.**

4 Color the **little bag blue.**

5 Color the **long snake pink.**

6 Color the **short snake purple.**

2 What color…?

1 The little apple is _____ red. _____

2 The big bag is _____

3 The long snake is _____

4 The big apple is _____

5 The little bag is _____

6 The short snake is _____

Connect the matching letters.

I   k

J   i

K   l

L   j

Write the letters.

I   i

J   j

K   k

L   l

Say the words, color and write.

I i → blue   J j → yellow   K k → green   L l → orange

 I i

 J j

 K k

 L l

27

1 Whose...?

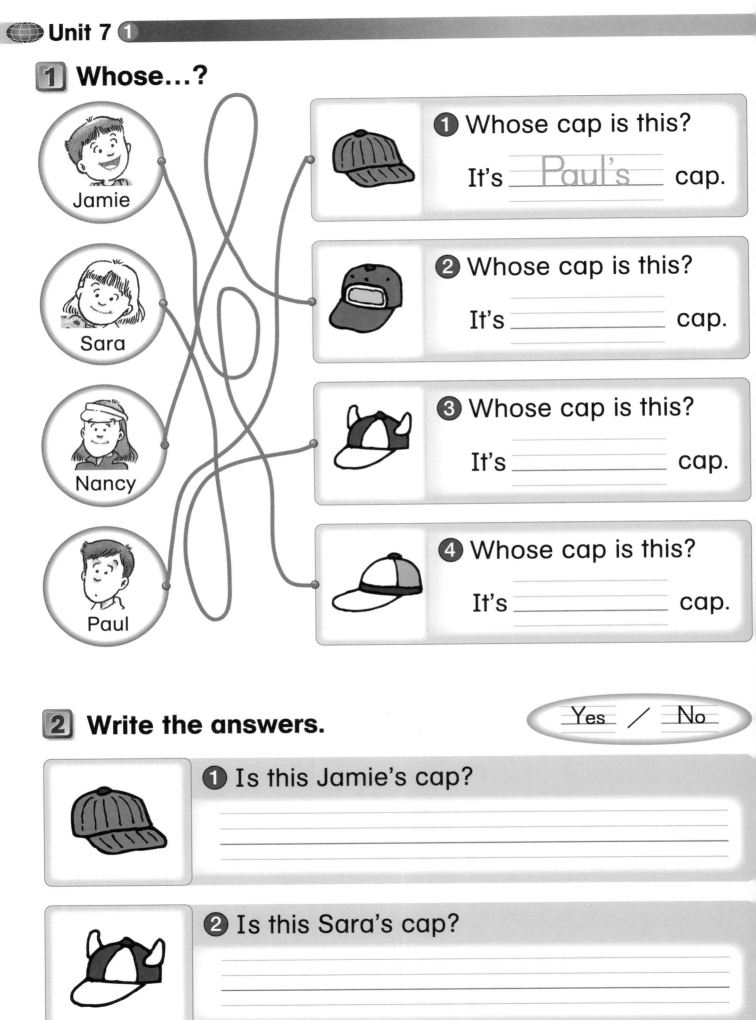

Jamie

Sara

Nancy

Paul

① Whose cap is this?

It's ___Paul's___ cap.

② Whose cap is this?

It's _____ cap.

③ Whose cap is this?

It's _____ cap.

④ Whose cap is this?

It's _____ cap.

2 Write the answers.

Yes / No

① Is this Jamie's cap?

_____

② Is this Sara's cap?

_____

Color and write.

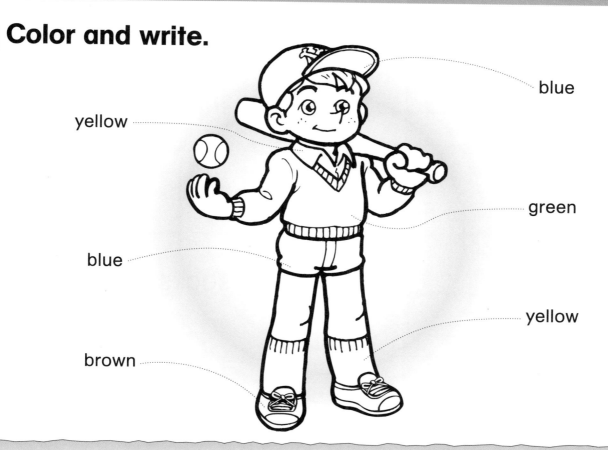

blue

yellow

green

blue

yellow

brown

Sam

① His ___cap___ is _____.

② His ___shirt___ is _____.

③ His ___sweater___ is _____.

④ His ___shorts___ are _____.

⑤ His ___socks___ are _____.

⑥ His ___sneakers___ are _____.

cap   shirt   sweater   shorts   socks   sneakers

1 Color and write.

1. I like a _____ shirt.

2. I like _____ pants.

3. I like _____ socks.

4. I like a _____ sweater.

5. I like _____ shoes.

2 Draw flowers.

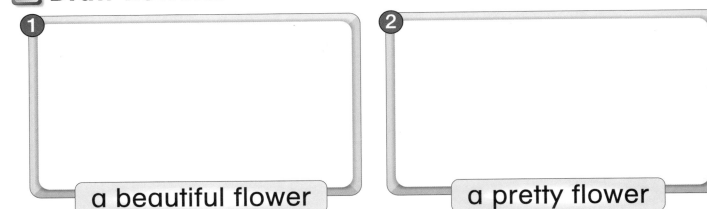

1. a beautiful flower

2. a pretty flower

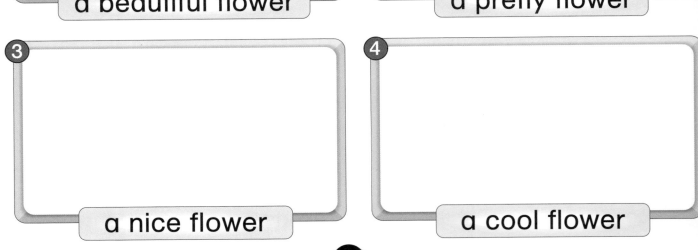

3. a nice flower

4. a cool flower

Connect the matching letters.

M   n

N   o

O   p

P   m

Write the letters.

M   m

N   n

O   o

P   p

Say the words, color and write.

Mm → green   Nn → orange   Oo → red   Pp → blue

 M m

 N n

 O o

 P p

1 **Choose and circle.**

1 He is
a teacher.
a scientist.

2 He is
a soccer player.
a baseball player.

3 She / He
is a doctor.

4 She / He
is a doctor.

2  He / She

1 _____ is a teacher.

2 _____ is a doctor.

⬜ Write your own.

can / can't

1 I _____ skate.

2 I _____ swim.

3 I _____ play the piano.

4 I _____ cook.

5 I _____ ski.

6 I _____ climb a tree.

Word Search

① JAMIE ② PAUL ③ BINGO

④ SARA ⑤ TERRY ⑥ NANCY

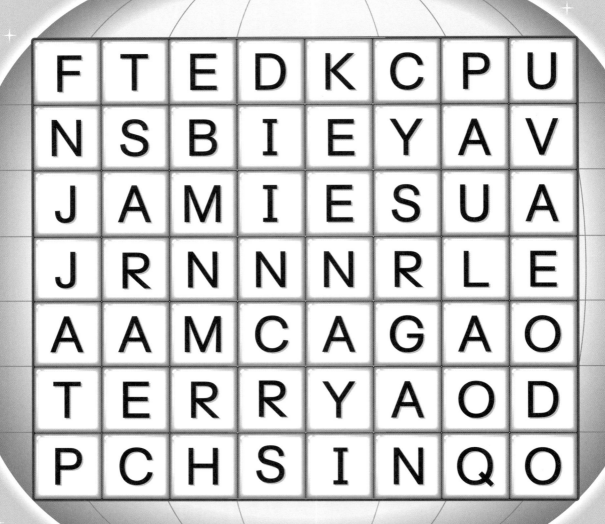

F	T	E	D	K	C	P	U
N	S	B	I	E	Y	A	V
J	A	M	I	E	S	U	A
J	R	N	N	N	R	L	E
A	A	M	C	A	G	A	O
T	E	R	R	Y	A	O	D
P	C	H	S	I	N	Q	O

Look at the words in the box.
Find them in the puzzle and circle them.

Connect the matching letters.

Q   r

R   t

S   u

T   s

U   q

Write the letters.

Q   q

R   r

S   s

T   t

U   u

Say the words, color and write.

Qq → blue   Rr → green   Ss → orange   Tt → red   Uu → pink

   Q q      R r

   S s

   T t      U u

Write the correct month.

1 The 1st month is _____

2 The 2nd month is _____

3 The 3rd month is _____

4 The 4th month is _____

5 The 5th month is _____

6 The 6th month is _____

7 The 7th month is _____

8 The 8th month is _____

9 The 9th month is _____

10 The 10th month is _____

11 The 11th month is _____

12 The 12th month is _____

The Twelve Months of the Year

January	February	March	April	May	June	July
August	September	October	November	December		

1 How many …?

 =10

1

2

3

2 Write the answers.

1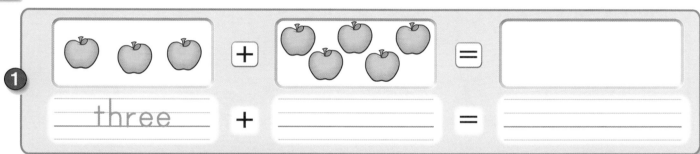

three + ___ = ___

2

___ + ___ = ___

3

___ + ___ = ___

4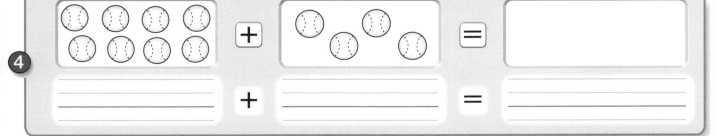

___ + ___ = ___

1 Color the pencils and write.

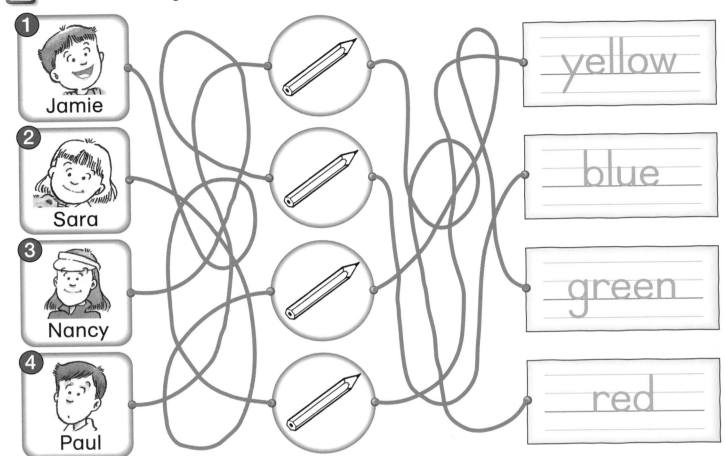

yellow

blue

green

red

2 What color…?

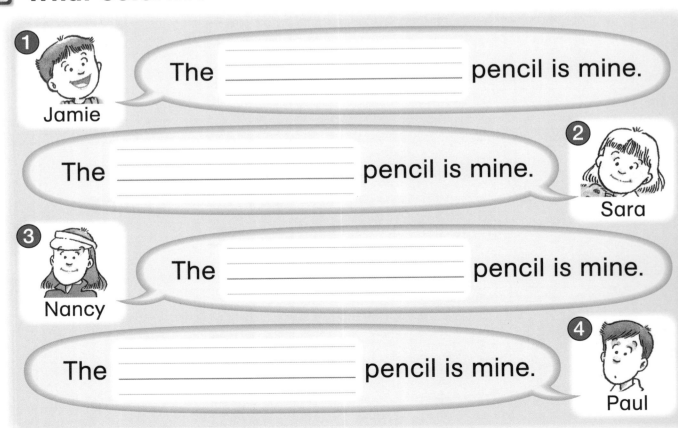

1 Jamie
The _____ pencil is mine.

2 Sara
The _____ pencil is mine.

3 Nancy
The _____ pencil is mine.

4 Paul
The _____ pencil is mine.

Connect the matching letters.

V   Z

W   y

X   x

Y   v

Z   W

Write the letters.

V   v

W   w

X   x

Y   y

Z   z

Say the words, color and write.

Vv → blue   Ww → yellow   Xx → green   Yy → orange   Zz → red

    V v       W w

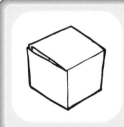    X x

    Y y      Z z

1 **What time is it?**

It's ___ : ___ .

It's ___ : ___ .

It's ___ : ___ .

It's ___ : ___ .

It's ___ : ___ .

It's ___ : ___ .

2 **Write the answer and read the formula.**

1 10 + 15 = [ ]

2 26 + 13 = [ ]

3 11 + 11 = [ ]

4 32 + 18 = [ ]

Say the words and color.

animals → red   food → purple

fruit → yellow

1 bird

2 peach

3 tiger

4 cake

5 turtle

6 salad

7 dog

8 banana

9 pancakes

10 horse

11 apple

12 hippo

13 elephant

14 ostrich

15 cheese

16 spaghetti

17 duck

18 blueberry

19 giraffe

20 cat

21 dinosaur

22 monkey

23 bear

24 grapefruit

25 pizza

26 orange

27 fox

28 lion

29 fried chicken

30 rabbit

⬤ Circle the correct answer.

1 Look at the boy.

My name is Jim.
I am 8 years old.   I can ski.

❶ What's his name?

| His |
| Her | name is Jim.

❷ How old is Jim?

| He |
| She | is _____ years old.

❸ What can Jim do?

| He |
| She | can _____ .

2 Look at the girl.

❶ What's her name?

| His |
| Her | name is Julie.

My name is Julie.
I am 9 years old.
I can swim.

❷ How old is Julie?

| He |
| She | is _____ years old.

❸ What can Julie do?

| He |
| She | can _____ .

1 Color the ship.

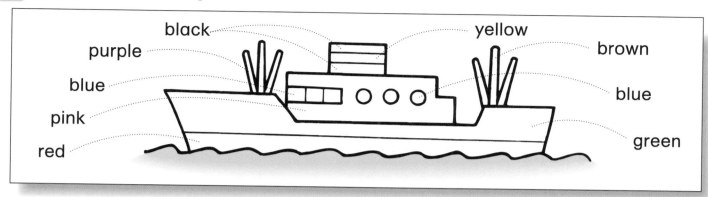

black .... yellow
purple .... brown
blue .... blue
pink ....
red .... green

2 What is the initial letter?

1
2
3
4
5
6

3 Circle the correct answer.

1. It **is / isn't** sunny today.

2. I **am / am not** a boy.

3. It is **Monday   Tuesday   Thursday   Wednesday   Friday   Saturday** today.

4. I **like / don't like** milk.

Read and color.

1 a red ant

2 a yellow sun

3 a green hat

4 a blue bag

5 an orange cat

6 a pink pig

7 a black jet

8 a brown dog

9 a white fox

10 a purple cap

11 two black cats

12 two yellow dogs

❶ Choose and circle.

❶ Santa Claus is happy.	left	right
❷ Santa Claus is angry.	left	right
❸ Santa Claus is big.	left	right
❹ Santa Claus is small.	left	right
❺ The Christmas tree is big.	left	right
❻ The Christmas tree is small.	left	right

❷ Color the pictures.

❶ The right Santa Claus is wearing a blue cap.

❷ The left Santa Claus is wearing a red cap.

❸ The right Christmas tree is red.

❹ The left Christmas tree is green.

1. Color the 🥕 orange.
   nose

2. Color the ○ ○ blue.
   eyes

3. Color the ▭ black.
   mouth

4. Color two 🍊🍊 red.
   oranges

5. Color three 🍊🍊🍊 yellow.
   oranges

6. Color the 🧤 green.
   mitten

7. Color the 🐕 brown.
   dog